Spiritual Keys for every Healing

David C. Hairabedian

Spiritual Keys for every Healing

David C. Hairabedian

© 2019 Virtual Church Media.com

1835 Newport Blvd

Building A-109, #333

Costa Mesa, CA 92627

Reproduction can be obtained with permission through
VirtualChurchMedia.com

Email: Info@VirtualChurchMedia.com

Phone: (949)648-1699

Contents

Spiritual Keys for Every Healing

Recently the Lord gave me a dream with a message concerning healing. He said, "There is a spiritual key for every healing." He emphasized strongly the word "every". Then He said the following words:

"For ALL who ask receive...not 70% or 80 or 90 or 95%, but ALL who ask believing, receive...ALL who seek shall find, and ALL who knock, the door shall be opened unto them...for I am no respecter of persons and My word is true ALL the time...there is a spiritual key for every healing."

Suddenly, several Scriptures began to pass through my mind, one after another. One dealt with forgiving others, another with fasting, others with obedience, and proper giving. The list went on and on as the Lord, by His grace, pried open my mind and filled it with spiritual keys to unlock the door for healings to enter into various people's lives. As the above Scriptures and keys were given, I also received a face to accompany each one. I realized that the healings the Lord spoke of were not only physical healings. They also included the healings of past hurts and wounds, deliverance from emotional torment, restoration of marriage situations, and a number of other things, including financial situations.

"For ALL who ask receive...not 70% or 80 or 90 or 95%, but ALL who seek shall find...for I am no respecter of persons...there is a spiritual key for every healing." The Lord then showed me a picture of the Body of Christ. It encompassed multitudes in need of healing, including many couples and ministers through whom the Lord's Hand of healing often flowed. The spiritual key for every healing need was shown clearly. What was surprising was the fact that, in some situations, it wasn't the one in need of healing who had the key, but the minister. The door for healing was shut because the minister wouldn't exercise his use of the key. For example, the Lord put a verse of Scripture (almost like a label

1

or a tag) above one minister's head that read "Mark 9:29": This kind can come forth by nothing, but by PRAYER and FASTING (KJV).

I knew instantly the way to unlock healing in this specific situation. The minister had to use his key by committing himself to prayer and fasting in behalf of a dear woman and her husband. But, he refused. Instead of admitting his shortcoming, he offered some theological excuses to the couple, then just shook his head. I saw the couple walk off confused, disheartened, and even feeling a little condemned. I felt anger toward the minister. Then I realized that I too had probably withheld the spiritual key for another's healing. I was also guilty of refusing to deny the flesh. I had failed to spend proper time praying and fasting for others' healing, marriage restoration, deliverance, and the like. I was no longer angry, but convicted of my own sin.

Another couple came forward and the label (or tag) appeared above the husband's head, "Mark 11:25-26"

> And whenever you stand praying, if you have anything against anyone, forgive him and let it drop (leave it, let it go), in order that your Father Who is in heaven may also forgive you your [own] failings and shortcomings and let them drop. But if you do not forgive, neither will your Father in heaven forgive your failings and shortcomings
>
> Mark 11: 25-26, AMP

Instantly I knew the key to his wife's healing lay in his willingness to forgive a person against whom he was harboring ill will. Again, it wasn't the individual needing healing who held the key in this situation, but the man to whom she was married. The Lord quickened me to two passages of Scripture:

> For this reason a man will leave his father and mother and be united to his wife, and they will become one flesh...if one part suffers, every part suffers with it...so that there should be no division in the body.

I began to examine myself, searching for any unforgiveness or ill will I had held against others. I realized that my unwillingness to forgive may be related to a loved one being unable to receive their healing key which had been in my hand the whole time!

With this, I began to see the individual members of the One Body of Christ far more closely related to one another than ever before. Then, this Scripture came to me:

> For as the body is one, and hath many members, and all the members of that one body, being many, are one body: so also is Christ...If the foot shall say, Because I am not the hand, I am not of the body; is it therefore not of the Body?

> 1 Corinthians 12:12, 15, KJV

With this, I realized the responsibility we have one towards another as the One Body of Christ, and vowed a deeper commitment and conscious awareness to love all members equally. Another verse came to mind, confirming the importance of how we all receive from the Lord (our Head) through other members of His Body (His joints and ligaments):

> From him the whole body, joined and held together by every supporting ligament, grows and builds itself up in love, as each part does its work

> Ephesians 4:16, NIV

The Apostle Paul's words to the Church at Galatia rang in my spirit, "Bear one another's burdens, and so fulfill the law of Christ" (Galatians 6:2, NKJV).

This is not only a biblical principle, but also the very fulfillment of the law of Christ for every believer. Just as I began to ponder this, I heard another verse from the same passage, "For every man shall bear his own burden" (Galatians 6:5, WEB).

3

But Each Man Must Bear His Own Burden

Suddenly, I was shown a scene of innumerable people within the Body of Christ. They were walking around with tags of Scripture and labels of personal sins above their heads. And then, I realized that we are not only responsible to provide, when possible, the spiritual keys for others' healings, but we also have a responsibility for our own.

"For every man shall bear his own burden."

Galatians 6:5, WEB

"If we confess our sins, he is faithful and just to forgive us our sins, and cleanse us from all unrighteousness."

1 John 1:9, KJV

"But if we judged ourselves, we would not come under judgment."

1 Corinthians 11:31, NIV

"For this reason many of you are weak and ill, and some have died."

1 Corinthians 11:30, NRSV

Numerous Labels and Tags of Sin

I n the innumerable sea of souls, I saw, I remember several of the various tags of Scripture and labels of sin. One was labeled faultfinder/complainer (Jude 1:16). Another read disobedient to parents (2 Timothy 3:2). Yet another read half-hearted/lukewarm (Revelation 3:16). Other labels included the sins of pride, jealously, anger, resentment, bitterness, vanity, self-indulgence, lust, gluttony, witchcraft, judgmental, critical, robs God, forsakes fellowship, double-minded, legalism, and even religion.

The labels were numerous and covered everything under the sun. Many contained more than one label and verse. Some had so many they just seemed to overlap and could hardly be read, while others literally looked like inkblots. Just as I felt the latter was without hope, the Lord reminded me of the power of His Blood to cleanse ALL sin. Then I heard the words that began the dream; "There is a spiritual key for every healing." Again, He emphasized every. With this, I woke up.

After Awaking

After awaking from the dream, I pondered all I had been shown and my heart became even more convicted and broken before the Lord. His desire is to heal his people in every situation. However, in many cases, His children have missed the key to unlock Heaven's door. In some situations, it is another member of the Body who holds the key, but refuses to exercise it in behalf of the person in need.

As in the earlier examples, the minister who was unwilling to fast and pray for one of the sheep under his care or the husband who was unwilling to use his key of forgiveness so his wife could be healed. In other situations, it is the individual who holds the key to their own healing, deliverance, marriage restoration, or miracle. But they are unwilling, or unaware of how, to exercise the use of the key they possess. For most, it is simple repentance that would unlock the door. For others, they must release what they are holding on to before they can receive the key that God wants to give them.

It isn't that God is withholding anything from any of His children, it is His children who are refusing to take and exercise use of the keys that He has already provided for them. Two more verses came to mind:

> As his divine power has given to us all things that pertain to life and godliness, through the knowledge of Him who called us by glory and virtue: Whereby are given to us exceedingly great and precious promises: that through these you may be partakers of the divine nature, having escaped the corruption that is in the world through lust.
>
> 2 Peter 1:3-4, NKJV

> Therefore, since a promise remains of entering His rest, let us fear lest any of you should come short of it. For indeed the gospel was preached to us as well as to them; but the

word which they heard did not profit them, not being mixed with faith in those who heard it.

Hebrews 4:1-2, NKJV

I realized that God's provision for healing has already been made. It is for ALL of his children who will exercise their keys by taking God's precious promises and mixing them with faith. With this, I was brought into remembrance of various Old Testament accounts of God's willingness to heal even after judgment had come from His own mouth. King Hezekiah was the first that came to mind:

> In those days Hezekiah became ill and was at the point of death. The prophet Isaiah... went to him and said, "This is what the LORD says: Put your house in order, because you are going to die; you will not recover."

2 Kings 20:1, NIV

Hezekiah, a righteous man, exercised use of the spiritual key in his hand before the Lord, unlocking the door to not only healing, but also an additional fifteen years of life:

> Hezekiah turned his face to the wall and prayed to the LORD, "Remember, O LORD, how I have walked before you faithfully and with wholehearted devotion and have done what is good in your eyes." And Hezekiah wept bitterly.

2 Kings 20:2-3, NIV

When God saw Hezekiah's prayer and tears, Heaven's mind changed in an instant, and the prophecy of death was reversed into a prophecy of healing, life extension, deliverance, and protection:

> Before Isaiah had left the middle court, the word of the LORD came to him: "Go back and tell Hezekiah, the leader of my people, 'This is what the LORD, the God of your father David, says: I have heard your prayer and seen your tears; I will heal you. On the third day from now you will go

up to the temple of the LORD. I will add fifteen years to your life. And I will deliver you and this city from the hand of the king of Assyria. I will defend this city for my sake and for the sake of my servant David.'"

2 Kings 20:4-6, NIV

Hezekiah's prayer and heartfelt tears were the spiritual key that unlocked not only healing for him, but also life extension of fifteen years, deliverance of an entire nation from the Assyrian army and divine protection from God.

"On the very day I call to you for help, my enemies will retreat. This I know: God is on my side...You have collected all my tears in your bottle. You have recorded each one in your book".

Psalms 56:9, 8, NLT

"Those who sow in tears will reap with songs of joy"

Psalms 126:5, NIV

Often, our heartfelt prayers, accompanied by tears of brokenness ["I have heard your prayer and seen your tears"] prove to be the spiritual key to healing ["I will heal you...I will add fifteen years...I will deliver you...and defend this city..."] (2 Kings 20:4-6, NIV).

Then I thought of all the times I had only sought God in a half-hearted manner for healing, deliverance, or the like, but rarely ever wept bitterly before Him with total brokenness and a contrite spirit. It became apparent to me why healing or answers to my prayers had often been delayed. It wasn't always the devil who'd been the hindrance, but me.

"God opposes the proud, but gives grace to the humble"

James 4:6, NKJV

With this, I remembered the story of King Asa:

> In the thirty-ninth year of his reign Asa was afflicted with a disease in his feet. Though his disease was severe, even in his illness he did not seek help from the LORD, but only from the physicians. Then in the forty-first year of his reign Asa died and rested with his fathers.
>
> 2 Chronicles 16:12-13, NIV

King Asa, a righteous man, refused to seek the Lord during his time of sickness, but instead put more trust and hope in the physicians of his day.

> "Cursed is the one who trusts in man, who depends on flesh for his strength and whose heart turns away from the LORD"
>
> Jeremiah 17:5, NIV

I wondered if it wasn't God's desire to heal Asa and extend his days like King Hezekiah. However, Asa's pride and self-sufficiency had kept heaven's doors locked tight. Then I studied Asa's name in the original Hebrew. Literally translated, Asa means physician. Asa's sin was trusting in himself rather than God. The problem wasn't that Asa sought the physicians for medical treatment (there is certainly nothing wrong with going to a doctor; God uses doctors), but Asa "did not seek help from the LORD, but only from the physicians" (2 Chronicles 16:12, NIV).

Many times when praying for the sick, I've recognized this same mindset in those needing healing. They trust first in the doctors instead of the Lord.

(Although they would never admit it openly, God isn't fooled).

> "But I know! I, the Lord, search all hearts and examine secret motives. I give all people their due rewards, according to what their actions deserve."
>
> Jeremiah 17:10, NLT

I wondered how many marriages could have been restored if the couple would have simply sought the Lord instead of the marriage counselors. Or sought the Lord first and the marriage counselors, lawyers, anti-depressant medications, etc...second.

> "But seek ye first the kingdom of God, and his righteousness; and all these things shall be added unto you."
>
> Matthew 6:33, KJV

So often we've sought things in reverse order. Things, things, things, and then the Lord afterwards. Could it be that, at times, we've even missed the mark by seeking healing first instead of first seeking the Healer; marriage restoration instead of the Marriage Restorer; deliverance instead of the Deliverer; finances instead of the Financial Provider? Have we sought what is in God's Hand, instead of what is in His Heart?

King Hezekiah's heart broke before the Lord as he wept bitterly. When Hezekiah's heart changed, God's heart towards him changed also...

> "Before Isaiah had left the middle court, the word of the LORD came to him...tell Hezekiah...I have heard your prayer and seen your tears...I will heal you..."
>
> 2 Kings 20:4-5, NIV

Divine Timing Can Play a Role in Our Healing

In Hezekiah's case God responded immediately to his request and healed him on the third day (2Kings 20:5). What do we do when the heavens seem to be brass and no sign of healing or answer comes from God for weeks, months, or even years?

Don't give up! Don't lose hope! God's delays are not God's denials. The story of the man at the Gate Beautiful (from the Book of Acts) came to mind.

There was divine timing involved in this miracle from God, which resulted in an even greater miracle, affecting the lives of thousands of others. Let's take a look:

> One day Peter and John were going up to the temple at the time of prayer – at three in the afternoon. Now a man crippled from birth was being carried to the temple gate called Beautiful, where he was put every day to beg from those going into the temple courts. When he saw Peter and John about to enter, he asked them for money. Peter looked straight at him, as did John. Then Peter said, "Look at us!" So the man gave them his attention, expecting to get something from them. Then Peter said, "Silver or gold I do not have, but what I have I give you. In the name of Jesus Christ of Nazareth, walk." Taking him by the right hand, he helped him up, and instantly the man's feet and ankles became strong. He jumped to his feet and began to walk. Then he went with them into the temple courts, walking and jumping, and praising God.
>
> Acts 3:1-8, NIV

In this passage, the man at the gate had been crippled from birth.

He'd waited on his healing all his life. But at the appointed hour, God sent Peter and John with the healing anointing that changed his life. What's not mentioned directly in this passage is the fact that Jesus walked by this man daily for three and a half years and never healed him. How do we know this?

Jesus was teaching and preaching in the temple daily during his ministry on earth (see Matthew 26:55). For Jesus to get into the temple, he would have had to walk right by the lame man through the Beautiful Gate. Why didn't Jesus heal him on any one of those given days? Could it be that this man's miracle was appointed for a special purpose that would affect the eternal souls of others?

The next chapter records that because of this great miracle five thousand men believed in Jesus (see Acts 4:1-4). Sometimes our miracles are delayed for a season because God has a greater purpose in accomplishing them. But don't give up hope, even if it seems that Jesus has passed you by for years. Because at the appointed hour, the miracle will come your way, possibly from an unexpected source, as it did for the lame man at the gate.

> "There is a time and a season for everything under the sun...a time to heal."
>
> Eccesiastes 3:1-3

If there is a divine timing for certain miracles from Heaven, is it also possible for us to miss our miracle? The following passage may shed some light:

> And it came to pass on a certain day, as Jesus was teaching, that there were Pharisees and doctors of the law sitting by, which were come out of every town of Galilee, and Judea, and Jerusalem: and the power of the Lord was present to heal them.
>
> Luke 5:17, KJV

Here we see God's power present to heal them. Yet, as the passage continues, we discover that none of them got healed! How could this be?

They missed their hour of visitation from the Lord. Instead, they were more interested in arguing doctrine and questioning the healer's authority.

> And the Scribes and the Pharisees began to reason, saying, Who is this which speaketh blasphemies? Who can forgive sins, but God alone?
>
> Luke 5:21, KJV

Jesus demonstrated who he was and healed an uninvited man with palsy who'd been lowered through the tiles in the ceiling of the home:

> But when Jesus perceived their thoughts, He answered and said to them, "Why are you reasoning in your hearts? Which is easier, to say, 'Your sins are forgiven you,' or to say, Rise up and walk'?
>
> But that you may know that the Son of Man has power on earth to forgive sins," He said to the man who was paralyzed, "I say to you, arise, take up your bed, and go to your house." Immediately he rose up before them, took up what he had been lying on, and departed to his own house, glorifying God. And they were all amazed, and they glorified God and were filled with fear, saying, "We have seen strange things today!"
>
> Luke 5:22-26, NKJV

Often God's children can become too intellectual in their reasoning at the wrong hour. I'm not suggesting we shouldn't "test the spirits" (1 John 4:1) and "study to show ourselves approved unto God" (2 Timothy 2:15). Not at all, for we should. At the same time, let us beware that we don't get too theological at the wrong time and miss our hour of visitation from God as did the Scribes and Pharisees.

Sometimes we are on our knees (in prayer) whenour spiritual key to healing is being on our toes, discerning the times and seasons of God's moving in our midst.

> "And the power of God was present to heal them."
>
> Luke 5:17, KJV

> "For we also have had the gospel preached to us, just as they did; but the message they heard was of no value to them, because those who heard did not combine it with faith."
>
> Hebrews 4:2, NIV

Two things are worth noting here: (1) The power of God was present to heal them, but instead an uninvited guest who destroyed the roof of the home got healed by this same power; and (2) the uninvited guest's spiritual key to unlock healing was in his friends' hands who brought him to the gathering:

> And when they could not find by what way they might bring him in because of the multitude, they went upon the housetop, and let him down through the tiling with his couch into the midst before Jesus.
>
> Luke 5:19, KJV

Sometimes healing for others is in our hands, with a ride to a church service, a healing crusade, or a cell group meeting at a home. If we'll simply bring them to the meeting where God's power is present to heal, God will do the rest. "There is a spiritual key for every healing."

Chronos Time and Kairos Moments

In the original Greek, there are at least two distinct words for time used in the Scriptures. Chronos (general process of time, or chronological time) and Kairos (strategic, opportune, or right time, now time).

Chronos time (Strong's #5550); time as succession or measurement of moments as in chronometer, a meter of chronos); of the passing moments without any moral impact as to the opportunity and accomplishment in that time. Chronos has only length, not challenge of accomplishment, as Kairos.

Kairos (Strong's #2540), the time of opportunities. Chronos embraces all possible Kairos, and is often used as the larger and more inclusive term, but not the converse (see Kairos time, Acts 3:19; and Chronos time, Acts 3:21).

In the story above, the Pharisees and the Doctors of the Law witnessed the uninvited guest get healed instantly. There can be little question that this was not just any ordinary (chronos) day at the office. Instead, this was a special visitation of the Lord's presence, or a divine (kairos) moment.

Contained within the general (chronos) time of the evening came the special (kairos) moment ("and the power of God was present to heal them," Luke 5:17). But as Jesus said later in the same book, "they did not recognize their day of visitation" (Luke 19:44).

Often in a Church service (chronos, general time), there comes a special (kairos, opportune, strategic) moment where God's power is present for a specific purpose. It may be for healing, or deliverance, or possibly salvation.

There is a divine timing or order of things by the Spirit of God. Two things can occur during these "kairos" moments within the "chronos" service: (1) those the Lord desires to touch can respond during the kairos opportunity and receive their breakthrough, touch, miracle, etc., or (2) they can resist, and miss their day of visitation as did the Pharisees and Scribes.

Some of the reasons God's children often miss their day (hour, moment, kairos time) of visitation may include: offense towards the pastor, pride (not wanting to go to the altar in front of others), intellectualism, disbelief, self-logic ("God doesn't work this way. Besides, if He wanted to heal me, He could heal me right here in my seat."), and the like. In these situations, the spiritual key to healing appears to simply be "obedience to step into the water when it is stirred" (see John 5:7) during these Kairos moments. For Blind Bartimaeus, it was simply "calling to Jesus when he was passing by"

(Mark 10:46-52).

In Bartimaeus' situation, he had to cry out even louder over the objections of the crowd who had "charged him to hold his peace" (vs .48). Bartimaeus recognized his day of visitation and received his sight from the Master during this Kairos (strategic, opportune) moment when Jesus was passing by.

Zacchaeus, the rich chief of the publicans, recognized his spiritual day of visitation, running in front of the others, climbing up into a sycamore tree to get a better view of this Jesus (Luke 19:1-10). Jesus called him down from the tree to eat at his house that day (vs. 5). Zacchaeus responded by coming down out of the tree, repenting of his past fraudulent financial dealings, (restoring fourfold to all he had defrauded) , and "giving half of his goods unto the poor" (vs. 8). Zacchaeus exercised use of the keys to his salvation in his hands during this Kairos moment and Jesus responded: "This day is salvation come to this house..." (vs. 9).

For Naaman, his key was "washing seven times in the Jordan River"

(2 Kings 5:1-19) during a Kairos moment. At first, he was offended by the command (vs. 11), and like the Pharisees and Scribes, almost missed his day of visitation during this Kairos opportunity. But then, after being counseled by a servant, he "stepped into the waters and was made whole" (vs. 14).

Have there been Kairos opportunities in days gone by that perhaps you have missed? Have you been invited to a special healing service, or meeting, and not responded. Has someone offered prayer through the laying on of hands and you've not allowed them? Was it an altar call at a service when you sensed the Lord calling you forward to touch the hem of his garment, but you allowed the opportunity to pass you by, just sitting in your seat? Could it be "restoring fourfold to those you may have defrauded," or "giving half your goods unto the poor" when Jesus calls you down from your high place out of your tree? Maybe you did call on Jesus, but the religious folks charged you to hold your peace and not bother the Master (Mark 10:48), and you fell silent. Could it be that you should have pressed through and cried all the louder like Bartimaeus until you received your miracle during your day of visitation and strategic Kairos moment with Jesus?

The good news is, it's not too late. God loves you so much that he is already setting up another Kairos moment for you. His nature is to redeem the time because the days are evil. In fact, this teaching hasn't fallen into your hands by accident. Jesus is already at work, preparing your Kairos moment with Him as we speak. This time you'll be able to recognize it when it comes and step into the waters when your hour of visitation occurs!

Partial Healings?

D o healings from Heaven sometimes come in parts or stages? If so, why? For example, why does Scripture record an instance where Jesus prayed for the same man twice for healing? And why did he receive a partial healing the first time, and then a full healing on the second go-round? Let's examine the following passage together:

> Then He came to Bethsaida; and they brought a blind man to Him, and begged Him to touch him. So, He took the blind man by the hand and led him out of the town. And when He had spit on his eyes and put His hands on him, He asked him if he saw anything. And he looked up and said, "I see men like trees, walking." Then He put His hands on his eyes again and made him look up. And he was restored and saw everyone clearly.
>
> Mark 8:22-25, NKJV

I believe this passage is included in the Gospels as encouragement to God's children. Sometimes we have to pray for someone more than once before their healing is fully manifest. At other times, healings are instantaneous.

And still at other times, healings are delayed, or come in stages. The message here may be:

> "ask and keep on asking...for God is a rewarder of those who diligently seek after him...for you shall seek me and find me when you search for me with all your heart."
>
> Matthew 7:7; Hebrews 11:6; Jeremiah 29:13

Persistence pays off and often God gives us a touch here and a touch there to encourage us to follow after Him. Moreover, faith for miracles often grows from one experience with Him to the next. We grow from grace to grace, faith to faith, and glory to glory in His presence.

Healed or Made Whole?

The story of the ten lepers gives a distinction between healing and being made whole:

> And it came to pass, as he went to Jerusalem, that he passed through the midst of Samaria and Galilee. And as he entered into a certain village, there met him ten men that were lepers, which stood afar off: And they lifted up their voices, and said, Jesus, Master have mercy on us. And when he saw them, he said unto them, Go show yourselves unto the priests. And it came to pass, that, as they went, they were cleansed. And one of them, when he saw that he was healed turned back and with a loud voice glorified God, And fell down on his face at Jesus' feet, giving Him thanks: and he was a Samaritan. And Jesus answering said, Were there not ten cleansed? but where are the nine? There are not found that returned to give glory to God, save this stranger. And he said unto him, Arise, go thy way: thy faith has made thee whole.
>
> Luke 17:11-19, KJV

In the above passage, we see ten lepers exercising their spiritual key for healing by simply calling on Jesus for mercy, acknowledging him as Master (vs. 13). Jesus commands them to go show themselves to the priests (vs. 14). Scripture records, that as they were obedient to the word of Jesus, the healing began. ("And it came to pass, that, as they went, they were cleansed.") Sometimes, healings don't begin to manifest (or fully lay hold) until we obey (do) what God commands us. For example, Jesus often asked someone to do something they couldn't do to release their healing into action. "Stretch forth your hand...rise up and walk...pick up your bed...go wash in the river ...put a clump of figs on the boil...go show yourselves to the priests...etc." "God's commands are not too hard for us" (1 John 5:3, SIM) and with the commandment, he also releases grace to do what he asks.

Obedience is faith in action. In many instances, if we will do as the Lord commands, we will experience the miracles He promises us.

Of the ten lepers who were cleansed, only one returned to Jesus to give thanks to God, falling at Jesus' feet and worshiping (vs. 16). This was the spiritual key that unlocked a second dimension to this leper's restoration, making him completely whole (vs. 19).

It is worth noting that leprosy in its progressive form often results in paralysis, wasting of muscle, deformities, mutilations, and even loss of extremities and body parts. The one leper was not only healed from the acid-fast bacterium infection, but also the results it had caused, making him totally restored and completely whole. It was a two-step process, exercising two different spiritual keys to deliverance, healing and new life in Christ.

It could be argued that calling on Jesus for mercy and acknowledging Him as Master, can often be the spiritual key to unlock Heaven's door for healing.

While returning to give him thanks, falling down at his feet in worship, is the spiritual key to bring total restoration (spirit, soul and body, with everlasting life).

Of all the people Jesus healed during his earthly ministry, how many were waiting for him on the day of Pentecost in the upper room? Only 120. Often, we get something from the Father's hand and run back to the world with it.

It might be our health, our marriage, our deliverance from crisis, a financial situation, or the like. God has so much more for us if we'll just turn back and give Him thanks and worship Him.

"Men ought to always pray and not lose heart."

Luke 18:1, NKJV

Can Our Land Be Healed?

Then it occurred to me that perhaps Sodom and Gomorrah could have been saved if just ten men would have repented, sparing the entire city (see Genesis 18:32). This made me think about our own nation, and how God's hand of judgment has been stayed (and even reversed) because of those who have faithfully prayed and fasted over the last several years and, in some cases, even decades. People prayed for almost thirty years before the Berlin wall came down. This opened the door for the gospel to flood in and bring multitudes to Christ.

The story of Jonah and the wicked city of Nineveh came to mind:

> On the first day, Jonah started into the city. He proclaimed: "Forty more days and Nineveh will be overturned." The Ninevites believed God. They declared a fast, and all of them, from the greatest to the least, put on sackcloth...When God saw what they did and how they turned from their evil ways, he had compassion and did not bring upon them the destruction he had threatened.
>
> Jonah 3:4-5, 10, NIV

When the people changed their hearts, the Bible records that God saw their works, that they turned from their evil ways. As a result, Heaven changed its heart towards them.

> "...he (God) had compassion and did not bring upon them the destruction he had threatened."
>
> Jonah 3:10, NIV

Corporate Fasting

orporate fasting turned the war around in the day of King Jehoshaphat (2 Chronicles 20), saving the people of Judah. Corporate fasting saved the people of Israel from total extermination during the days of Esther and Mordecai (Esther Chapters 4-9).

And the Book of Isaiah offers almost an entire chapter on the benefits of seeking the Lord through prayer and fasting:

> ...is not this the fast that I have chosen to loose the bonds of wickedness, to undo the bands of the yoke, to let the oppressed go free, and that you break every [enslaving] yoke?..Then shall your light break forth like the morning, and your healing (your restoration and the power of a new life) shall spring forth speedily; your righteousness (your rightness, your justice, and your right relationship with God) shall go before you [conducting you to peace and prosperity], and the glory of the Lord shall be your rear guard. Then you shall call, and the Lord will answer; you shall cry, and He will say, Here I am...
>
> Isaiah 58:6-9, AMP

Then I remembered God's promise to His people during the days of Jeremiah:

> For I know the plans I have for you," declares the LORD, "plans to prosper you and not to harm you, plans to give you hope and a future. Then you will call upon me and come and pray to me, and I will listen to you. You will seek me and find me when you seek me with all your heart.
>
> Jeremiah 29:11-13, NIV

And His promise to the children of Israel during the days of

Solomon:

> If My people, who are called by My name, shall humble
> themselves, pray, seek, crave, and require of necessity My
> face and turn from their wicked ways, then will I hear from
> heaven, forgive their sin and heal their land.

2 Chronicles 7:14, AMP

Ask and Keep on Asking...Seek and Keep on Seeking...

Again, I remembered the words with which the dream began.

"For ALL who ask receive...not 70% or 80 or 90 or 95%, but ALL who ask believing receive...ALL who seek shall find, and ALL who knock the door shall be opened unto them...for I am no respecter of persons and My Word is true ALL the time...there is a spiritual key for every healing."

Knowing this message was based on Scripture from the Gospel of Matthew (Jesus' Sermon on the Mount), I looked it up and began to study it afresh:

> ASK and it shall be given you; SEEK, and ye shall find; KNOCK and it shall be opened. For everyone that asketh receiveth; and he that seeketh findeth, and to him that knocketh it shall be opened.
>
> Or what man is there of you, whom if his son ask bread, will he give him a stone? Or if he ask a fish, will he give him a serpent? If ye then, being evil, know how to give good gifts unto your children, how much more shall your Father which is in heaven give good things to them that ask him.
>
> Matthew 7:7-11, KJV

When taking a closer look at this oft quoted passage, one discovers that the words, ask, seek and knock are all in the present imperative tense in the original Greek. This indicates a command to do something now, with a constant, repeated action in the future until given the requested response.

The Amplified Version actually translates it this way:

"Keep on asking and it will be given you; keep on seeking

and you will find; keep on knocking [reverently] and [the door] will be opened to you. For everyone who keeps on asking receives; and he who keeps on seeking finds; and to him who keeps on knocking, [the door] will be opened."

Matthew 7:7-8, AMP

I began to realize that many of God's children (myself included) often give up too soon in prayer. We haven't understood the Biblical examples Jesus provided for us in the Gospels. For example, in the parable of the persistent widow and the unjust judge, Jesus taught this:

Then He spoke a parable to them, that men always ought to pray and not lose heart, saying: "There was in a certain city a judge who did not fear God nor regard man. Now there was a widow in that city; and she came to him, saying, 'Avenge me of my adversary.' And he would not for a while; but afterward he said within himself, 'Though I do not fear God nor regard man, yet because this widow troubles me I will avenge her, lest by her continual coming she weary me.'" Then the Lord said, "Hear what the unjust judge said. And shall God not avenge His own elect who cry out day and night to Him, though He bears long with them? I tell you that He will avenge them speedily. Nevertheless, when the Son of Man comes, will He really find faith on the earth?"

Luke 18:1-8, NKJV

This persistent widow Jesus spoke of is a perfect role model for 21st century believers.

"Men always ought to pray and not lose heart...because of her continual coming, I will avenge her."

Luke 18:1, 5

"Ask and keep on asking, seek and keep on seeking, knock

and keep on knocking..."

Matthew 7:7

"Let us fear lest a promise being left to us, any of you should come short of it."

Hebrews 4:1

"As His divine power has given to us all things..."

2 Peter 1:3

"The same word was preached unto us as unto them, but it profited them nothing, not being mixed with faith in them that heard it"

Hebrews 4:2

"There is a spiritual key for every healing...for ALL who ask receive... not 70% or 80 or 90 or 95%, but ALL who ask believing receive... ALL who seek [and keep on seeking] shall find...for God is no respecter of persons and His Word is true ALL the time..."

A second example in Scripture is the story of the Gentile woman who sought Jesus for healing in behalf of her daughter who was possessed with an evil spirit:

> And behold, a woman of Canaan came from that region and cried out to Him, saying, "Have mercy on me, O Lord, Son of David! My daughter is severely demon-possessed." But He answered her not a word. And His disciples came and urged Him, saying, "Send her away, for she cries out after us." But He answered and said, "I was not sent except to the lost sheep of the house of Israel."
>
> Then she came and worshiped Him, saying, "Lord, help me!" But He answered and said, "It is not good to take the children's bread and throw it to the little dogs." And she said, "True, Lord, yet even the little dogs eat the crumbs which fall from their masters' table." Then Jesus answered

and said to her, "O woman, great is your faith! Let it be to you as you desire." And her daughter was healed from that very hour.

Mathew 15:22-28 NKJV

"O woman, great is your faith! Let it be to you as you desire," was the response she received from Jesus when she persevered in prayer. It's interesting to note that she received four negative responses before finally receiving healing for her daughter on the fifth petition: Have mercy on me, O Lord, Son of David! My daughter is severely demon-possessed. But he answered her not a word (vs. 22). And His disciples came and urged Him, saying, Send her away, for she cries after us (vs. 23). But he answered and said, I was not sent except the house of Israel (vs. 24).

Then she came and worshiped him, saying, Lord, help me! But He answered and said, It is not good to take the children's bread and throw it to the little dogs (vs. 26). And she said, Yes, Lord, yet even the little dogs eat the crumbs which fall from the Master's table. Then Jesus answered her and said, O woman great is your faith! Let it be to you as you desire. (vs. 28)

"Ask and keep on asking, seek and keep on seeking, knock and keep on knocking. .For ALL who ask receive...not 70% or 80 or 90 or 95%, but ALL who ask believing receive...ALL who seek [and keep on seeking] shall find, and ALL who knock [and keep on knocking] the door shall be opened unto them...for I am no respecter of persons and My Word is true ALL the time...there is a spiritual key for every healing."

Summary

There is a spiritual key for every healing. Some keys are in your hand and can be used for you or another member of the Body of Christ. Some keys are in the Lord's hand, and He's waiting for us to come and ask Him for it. In some situations, He may require us to give Him something in exchange for use of the key. It may be confession of sin, forgiving someone who has wronged us, or letting go of what we've been holding on to so our hands (and hearts) can be free to receive the key of healing He so eagerly desires to give. He may require us to lay something at His feet. (Not that He needs anything, but that we need to give or relinquish). It may be fasting (or a change of diet, giving up foods that have been harming our bodies). It may be our time or just sitting at the Master's feet in silence.

We, like the Gentile woman above, may not receive our answer from the Lord instantly. Jesus may not even answer us a word right away. Other ministers we approach for prayer and healing may even tell us to go away.

At first, we may even hear Jesus respond that we're not deserving of the children's bread (although this isn't usually the case). But eventually, as is His nature and character, He will respond favorably and avenge us of our adversary, deliver our child from sickness, bondage or demon influence, restore our marriage and the like. Remember, even when He told the Gentile woman no and called her a dog, he healed her daughter when she persevered. Jesus not only healed her daughter, but also praised her for her faith! "Men ought to pray always and not lose heart." "There is a spiritual key for every healing." "Ask and keep on asking...for He is a rewarder of them who diligently seek him...you will find Me when you search for Me with ALL your heart!" God's delays are not God's denials. Don't lose heart. Don't give up hope. Your healing is on the way!

If you enjoyed this book and want more experience in the supernatural power of God to heal the sick, cast out devils and see the lost come to know Jesus, I highly recommend my book, What the Bible REALLY says about Speaking in Tongues. Available on Kindle and Amazon.

Praying in tongues privately gives you power to preach the gospel publicly.

Praying in tongues privately releases heaven's will into situations you don't even know about, but God does. This is the reason I encourage people to pray in tongues as often as they can throughout the day. "Pray without ceasing" (1Thessalonians 5:17).

May the Holy Spirit fill you to overflowing as you continue to passionately and expectantly seek Him and His will for your life and ministry.

May God richly bless you as you continue to seek His face daily and trust you with more and more of his wisdom, power, healing virtue, revelation and miracles to reach others with the love of Christ.

Author, David C. Hairabedian

David and Joanna Hairabedian

David and Joanna Hairabedian are co-founders of VirtualChurchMedia.com. They live in Southern, California. David is an author, teacher and conference speaker.

Joanna is a writer, singer, a Prophetic Psalmist. Together, they host a weekly TV Broadcast called, In His Presence, Where ALL Things are Possible. David teaches and Joanna plays piano and sings. People report receiving encouragement, deliverance, healing and a tangible Presence of the Lord while watching these programs.

To download their ministry mobile app and access their ministry on demand, visit VirtualChurchMedia.com

Contact Information

Virtual Church Media Inc

1835 Newport Blvd

Building A-109, #333

Costa Mesa, CA 92627

(949) 648-1699

Info@VirtualChurchMedia.com

Prayer@VirtualChurchMedia.com

HEART Prison Ministries

If you would be interested in reading more of David's or Jeff's teachings, or for speaking/preaching engagements, please contact HEART of America Prison Ministries at PO Box 1685 Independence, MO 64055 or visit our website www.HeartPrisonMinistries.org.

HEART Ministries provides leather-bound study Bibles, devotionals, Bible study courses, videos, and newsletters to inmates in over 1,000 prisons and jails nationally and internationally. As HEART grows in the future, we look forward to contributing to your ministry efforts in the areas of prevention, prisoner support, and aftercare.

HEART has a vision to become a clearinghouse for ministry resource materials for free use by chaplains and inmates across the nation.

HEART Publishing

HEART Publishing is the media subsidiary of HEART of America Prison Ministries. Our primary purpose is to provide Christ-centered educational material for our brothers and sisters behind prison walls.

To purchase a copy of David's autobiography, Jet Ride to Hell, Journey to Freedom, visit VirtualChurchMedia.com or Amazon.com

To learn more about how you can help change lives, one Bible at a Time, or to donate for Bibles for prisoners visit HeartPrisonMinistries.org.

Partnering with us to Help Raise of 12 Disciples a Year through our Bible a month program can be life changing for the prisoner as well as the supporter. Visit to learn more how you can be the answer to someone's prayers.

For additional teachings, video sermonettes, Christian resource materials, ministry updates, visit these sites:

www.VirtualChurchTV.com

www.HeartPrisonMinistries.org

www.DavidHairabedian.com

Made in the USA
Columbia, SC
25 May 2019